A Gift for

_____

From

_____

Date

_____

CLASS OF 2013

31 Days with God
FOR GRADS

Inspiring Devotions, Prayers, and Quotations

BARBOUR
PUBLISHING

© 2013 by Barbour Publishing, Inc.

Material taken and adapted from *The Word on Life* by Toni Sortor and Pamela McQuade.

Print ISBN 978-1-62029-716-2

eBook Editions:
Adobe Digital Edition (.epub) 978-1-62029-975-3
Kindle and MobiPocket Edition (.prc) 978-1-62029-974-6

All scripture quotations are taken from the King James Version of the Bible.

Published by Barbour Publishing, Inc., P.O. Box 719, Uhrichsville, Ohio 44683, www.barbourbooks.com

Our mission is to publish and distribute inspirational products offering exceptional value and biblical encouragement to the masses.

 Member of the
Evangelical Christian
Publishers Association

Printed in the United States of America.

Grad,
give God a month...
just see where He takes you!

These 31 easy-reading devotions provide help, hope, and a touch of humor for new graduates. Each day for an entire month, you'll be encouraged and energized by a meditation relating to a vital aspect of your future—ministry, God's guidance, peace of mind, friends, romance, self-control, work, and much more. Each reading will bring your thoughts back to the heavenly Father, who cares so much about you, and the life you're building.

Accompanied by inspiring prayers and quotations, practical tips, and lined space for recording your own thoughts, this book is the perfect way to celebrate the brand-new life God has called you to.

DAY 1

SEEKING THE TRUTH

*Keep that which is committed
to thy trust, avoiding profane and
vain babblings, and oppositions
of science falsely so called.*

1 TIMOTHY 6:20

Young adulthood is the time to decide what you do and do not believe to be true. It's a time to question everything, reject some old things, and embrace some new things. It's a time that makes parents worry, because they know you will be looking critically at their beliefs, too.

You have to do this. You can't blindly accept everything you hear. You have to make your own decisions and be prepared to live with them, or you'll be a wishy-washy nobody.

You also have to learn discernment. That's what Paul was warning Timothy about. Some positions must be taken on faith. All the talk in the world can't prove the unprovable, so look at everything carefully before you decide to embrace a stand—but realize that some things just have to be accepted on faith, not facts.

Father, no one seems
to agree on anything,
including faith. Give me
discernment and the courage
to stand by my beliefs,
even if I can't prove
they are correct.

We know the truth
not only by the reason
but also by the heart.
BLAISE PASCAL

THINK IT OVER

What things are you beginning to question?

What beliefs are you rejecting?

Which are you holding on to as truth?

All the strength and force
of man comes from his faith
in things unseen. He who
believes is strong; he who doubts
is weak. Strong convictions
precede great actions.

JAMES FREEMAN CLARKE

*Faith is the substance
of things hoped for,
the evidence
of things not seen.*

HEBREWS 11:1

REST FOR THE WEARY

Also I heard the voice of the Lord,
saying, Whom shall I send,
and who will go for us?
Then said I, Here am I; send me.
ISAIAH 6:8

Ever wish that you could rewrite that verse to say, "Here am I. Send someone else"? When you feel overloaded spiritually, even though you'd like to comply, opening yourself to full obedience to God is hard.

Maybe, you worry, if I give Him free rein, He'll send me to Timbuktu (or wherever your least-favorite place in the world is). How could I ever cope with that? you wonder.

If you're feeling overloaded, take your burden to God, and confess that you've been hanging on to it. Then drop it in His hands and run! Don't stick around to pull it back out of the hands of the great burden-lifter.

Then let Him lead you as you make decisions about ministries with which you're over-involved, family problems that someone else needs to handle, or commitments you may not need to take on. Pledge yourself to obedience and walk in your new freedom. Don't let that old burden trap you again!

Send me, Lord, wherever
You want me to go.
I know You'll give me
the strength I need.

Faith never knows where
it is being led, but it loves and
knows the One who is leading.

Oswald Chambers

THINK IT OVER

What commitments have you been hanging on to that you need to let go of?

Why have you found it hard to hand them over to God?

Now that your hands are empty, where do you think God is calling you?

The Bible commands us to rest. . .
what a generous and kind
God we have. We expect
marching orders, or hoops
to jump through. But God simply
says, "All right, this will be
challenging, but here's what
I want you to do: take a break."

Keri Wyatt Kent

*In returning and rest shall ye
be saved; in quietness and in
confidence shall be your strength.*

Isaiah 30:15

DAY 3

LOOKING FOR DIRECTION

For I know the thoughts that
I think toward you, saith the Lord,
thoughts of peace, and not of evil,
to give you an expected end.

JEREMIAH 29:11

We all have plans for our future, even if they're a little vague. We know whether we want to marry and have children, places we want to go, and things we hope to accomplish. Most of us are realistic about our plans, knowing some will work out and some won't. We also know our plans will change from year to year as we mature and see more of the world.

What we don't like is to have our plans blown out of the water and to have our lives take a sudden change of direction. There's nothing more frightening than losing the anchor that's been holding our life in place and being forced to start over again.

Fortunately, some of these disasters turn out to be blessings. Even when we have no idea which way to turn, the Lord knows where we're going and will keep us on the right path, even if the trip's a little bumpy.

Father, when my life
suddenly turns upside down,
I will trust in You to lead
me in the right direction.

Walk boldly and wisely. . . .
There is a hand above
that will help you on.

PHILIP JAMES BAILEY

THINK IT OVER

What disasters have you experienced that turned out to be blessings?

When have you felt directionless, only to later discover that God was leading you the entire time?

How does it make you feel knowing that God is keeping you on the right path?

Never think that Jesus has hidden away the riches of wisdom and knowledge, as in a treasure chest without a key, or of your way as a path without a light. Jesus, who is your wisdom, is guiding you, even when you can't see it.

Andrew Murray

I will bring the blind by a way that they knew not; I will lead them in paths that they have not known: I will make darkness light before them, and crooked things straight. These things will I do unto them, and not forsake them.

Isaiah 42:16

DAY 4

TAKING TIME TO PRAY

*When thou prayest,
enter into thy closet, and when
thou hast shut thy door, pray to
thy Father which is in secret.*
MATTHEW 6:6

Time got away from Amy that morning, and prayer seemed to be out of the question. Jumping in her car, she decided, *I'll just pray while I drive*.

As she started off, so did her prayer, but soon she got caught in traffic. Faced with the choice of having an accident or praying, she kept her mind on the road. Past the traffic, Amy turned again to prayer, only to lose track once more when she saw a sale sign on one of her favorite stores.

Sure, you can pray while you drive—maybe you should sometimes—but if that's the only time you spend with God, you won't be giving Him your best. After all, two seconds of prayer here and a minute there can't compete with solid time when God can answer you.

If you only talked to your friends while you drove, you couldn't give them your full attention, and your communication would get mixed up. It's the same with God.

Lord, I know I can pray when I drive,
but there are too many distractions to
make it my prayer room. My life includes
time to spend with You. Show me when it is.

🎓

Is prayer your steering
wheel or your spare tire?

Corrie ten Boom

THINK IT OVER

When is your scheduled prayer time?

What things tend to disrupt you, or what distractions do you cave in to during that quiet time?

What can you do to ensure those moments in God's presence are uninterrupted?

Prayer is a declaration of our
dependence on God. It isn't
something mechanical you do;
it is somewhere you go to meet
Someone you know.

JILL BRISCOE

*The LORD is nigh unto all
them that call upon him,
to all that call upon him in truth.*

PSALM 145:18

DAY 5

"PRETTY IS AS PRETTY DOES"

Judge not according to the appearance,
but judge righteous judgment.

JOHN 7:24

Our whole country is caught up in appearance today, almost to the point of making it an idol. We are consumed by the desire to be thin, to be beautiful, to dress with flair and style. All of these may be perfectly legitimate personal goals, but we can all too easily pervert them, try to impose them on others, and then judge everyone as unworthy who doesn't measure up.

Today the fit mock those who puff their way up the stairs. The beautiful recommend nose jobs. The tall look down on the small; those who look as if they need a good sandwich feel superior to those who have obviously had too many.

Jesus tells us to look beyond the surface—to judge actions, not appearances. We have no right to make our personal preferences the basis for judging the worthiness of others.

Father, just as I don't want to be judged
by my acceptance of some popular trend,
neither do I want to judge others by my own
personal preferences. Keep me sensitive to
the feelings of others and help me see the
true person beyond the surface.

I don't like that man.
I must get to know him better.
ABRAHAM LINCOLN

THINK IT OVER

What do you think is true beauty?

How do you keep yourself from getting caught up in striving to attain good looks?

What do you find in others when you look beneath their surface?

We sell ourselves short if we think that
the joy of the Lord can be captured
in a cosmetically whitened smile.

Jonathan Wilson-Hartgrove

*The Lord seeth not as man seeth;
for man looketh on the outward
appearance, but the Lord
looketh on the heart.*

1 Samuel 16:7

DAY 6

HEADING FOR HOLINESS

*Let us cleanse ourselves from all
filthiness of the flesh and spirit,
perfecting holiness in the fear of God.*

2 CORINTHIANS 7:1

Unless you plan to live the life of a hermit, this verse is going to give you problems. We live in a thoroughly contaminated world where it's difficult to be even a little holy, let alone perfectly holy.

Start with the most important fact, though: Your sins have already been forgiven. How do you thank someone for saving your life now and forever? By trying to be what He wants you to be. No, you are not going to do it perfectly. Yes, you will still sin. But you will also steer clear of situations that God disapproves of. You will treat your body as the holy temple of God, who lives in you, and you will treat others the way you want to be treated. It's a start, anyway, and this is one case where good intentions do count.

Father, I can never live my life in total
holiness, but I can show my thankfulness
and reverence for You in many ways.
Help me live my life in a way that will reflect
Your glory and mercy and eternal love.

How little people know who think
that holiness is dull. When one meets
the real thing, it is irresistible.

C. S. LEWIS

In what areas do you separate yourself from the world?

How does it feel knowing that your body is the temple of God?

How would your life change if you unconditionally loved others the same way God loves you—warts and all?

If you seek holiness of life,
I encourage you to make a good
friend of the sermon on the mount.

<small>RICHARD J. FOSTER</small>

*According as he hath chosen us in
him before the foundation of the world,
that we should be holy and without
blame before him in love.*

<small>EPHESIANS 1:4</small>

BE A BLESSING

If a brother or sister be naked, and destitute of daily food, and one of you say unto them, Depart in peace, be ye warmed and filled; notwithstanding ye give them not those things which are needful to the body; what doth it profit?

JAMES 2:15–16

Billions of dollars are spent in America every year on movies and other forms of entertainment. Meanwhile, the view in other areas of America is hardly "entertaining." Churches struggle financially, and some needy families only get help when their stories reach the six o'clock news. Is it any surprise our nation is in trouble?

If we gave as generously to God as we do to our entertainment, imagine the people who could be helped. Churches could expand ministries to the inner city and support ministries all over the world. There'd be enough money to help a struggling family get back on its feet.

There are even ways to help that don't require money. Recycle. Volunteer with a local charity or school. Donate clothes you don't need. These efforts make a big difference to the lives that are affected.

The blessings that come with generous giving can hardly be imagined. Let's start the blessings today.

Lord, make me understand what I can
and cannot do to help others in the world
today. Show me the small actions I can
take that will make a difference.

The manner of giving shows the character
of the giver more than the gift itself.

Johann Kaspar Lavater

THINK IT OVER

In what ways are you currently a blessing to others?

What kind of difference did that make in their lives?

How does it feel to share your gift of time, money, or service?

Seek the welfare of others. Find
out how you can be a blessing.
Pray for the city you live in right
now and its people, for its welfare
and your welfare. This is one of the
fundamental keys. As you become
a blessing, you set yourself
up to be blessed.

TONY EVANS

Come, ye blessed of my Father,
inherit the kingdom prepared for
you from the foundation of the world:
For I was an hungred, and ye gave me
meat: I was thirsty, and ye gave me drink:
I was a stranger, and ye took me in.

MATTHEW 25:34–35

DAY 8

MODEL OBEDIENCE

*In every work that he began in
the service of the house of God,
and in the law, and in the
commandments, to seek his God,
he did it with all his heart
and prospered.*

2 CHRONICLES 31:21

King Hezekiah was totally committed to the service of God, seeking His will and working wholeheartedly. As a result, he prospered.

The Bible doesn't say that Hezekiah had an easy time of it. If you read his whole story, you'll see he worked harder than today's corporate leaders ever do. There must have been days when he was sick of all the organizing, rebuilding, defending, and other chores that fall on a king. He'd solve one problem only to have six others appear. Hezekiah wasn't perfect, either. He and the whole kingdom were punished for their pride when Hezekiah neglected to give God the glory for a miracle.

He must have been a wise man to rule successfully for twenty-nine years. But remember, Hezekiah was twenty-five when he became king! What would happen if we committed our lives to God and wholeheartedly followed His will?

Lord, teach me to seek Your will with all my heart, and do it with the wisdom and enthusiasm of Hezekiah, the young king who was rewarded for his faithfulness.

On board iron vessels it is a common thing to see a compass placed aloft, to be as much away from the cause of aberration as possible: a wise hint to us to elevate our affections and desires. The nearer to God, the less swayed by worldly influences.

CHARLES SPURGEON

THINK IT OVER

In what ministries do you find yourself making half-hearted efforts?

How would your life be different if you sought God's will and served Him whole-heartedly?

What steps can you take to change your heart attitude?

Serving God is about doing—
doing with every fiber of your
passion and commitment.

BRUCE WILKINSON

*If from thence thou shalt seek the
LORD thy God, thou shalt find him,
if thou seek him with all thy heart
and with all thy soul.*

DEUTERONOMY 4:29

DAY 9

TURNING TIME

*And the sun stood still, and the moon
stayed, until the people had avenged
themselves upon their enemies. . . .
So the sun stood still in the midst of
heaven, and hasted not to go down
about a whole day.*

JOSHUA 10:13

Amazing—at a time when they needed it, God gave the children of Israel an extra full day of light! The sun and the moon cooperated with humanity's need because God declared it. We can't explain how it happened. Used to the regular rising of the sun and moon, we can't imagine things any other way. It must have also astonished the Amorites, whom Israel was attacking. Instead of getting away under the cover of night, they had to keep fighting.

Now we have an extra day that only comes once every four years. Unlike the Amorites, it's not a total surprise to us. How do we use the extra twenty-four hours?

Every day is important. God doesn't have to stop time to make it so. How will you use today?

Thank You, Lord, for another day to serve You. I want to make the most of it by showing someone Your love.

Place all the hours of this day quite simply at His disposal, and ask Him to make and keep you ready to do just exactly what He appoints.

FRANCES HAVERGAL

THINK IT OVER

Who or what is steering your day?

In what ways do you find yourself "killing" time?

How can you better use the time you are given
to seek and to serve God?

Submerge as much of your day as
you can, to make it your invisible keel,
by eliminating less important things.
You need time to look into the face
of God, time to read and study his
Word systematically, time to think
and plan for your life, time to praise,
time to intercede, time to get wisdom
for handling people and for
making decisions.

ANNE ORTLUND

*Seek ye first the kingdom of God,
and his righteousness; and all these
things shall be added unto you.*

MATTHEW 6:33

DAY 10

REMAINING PURE

For this is the will of God, even your sanctification, that ye should abstain from fornication: that every one of you should know how to possess his vessel in sanctification and honour; not in the lust of concupiscence, even as the Gentiles which know not God.

1 THESSALONIANS 4:3-5

Avoiding sexual immorality does not come naturally—it has to be learned—and there are very few teachers you can count on today. Society at large is pretty useless, issuing plenty of warnings about disease but little positive, practical advice for those struggling to lead a sanctified life.

So who is available to teach these lessons? The best teacher is God Himself, who can teach you what He expects through the Bible. Use a good concordance to look up verses about sex, love, marriage, and so forth. You can't obey laws you don't know exist, but all the laws are there in the Bible. Besides knowledge, God can give you the strength you will need to control your own body and to live a pure life. Ask for His help when you need it.

Father, thank You for guiding
me in all things. Forgive me when
I disappoint You, and give me
the strength I need to please You.

Opportunity may knock only once,
but temptation leans on the doorbell.

Unknown

THINK IT OVER

In what situations are you tempted to give in to lust?

What can you do to avoid such situations?

What can you do to develop boundaries in your relationship with a member of the opposite sex?

To combat this X-rated
environment in which we live,
you need to create your own
"department of homeland security."
<small>ADRIAN ROGERS</small>

*Wherewithal shall a young man
cleanse his way? by taking heed
thereto according to thy word.*
<small>PSALM 119:9</small>

DAY 11

TELLING TALENTS

*One generation shall praise thy
works to another, and shall declare
thy mighty acts. I will speak of the
glorious honour of thy majesty,
and of thy wondrous works*

PSALM 145:4-5

There was no Internet, no instant communication, in the days of David. Most people couldn't read or write. Traditions were taught to the next generation by the older generation through stories, songs, and dances, which were memorable and enjoyable ways to learn. The psalms and hymns of the church not only lifted people's spirits but also served as teaching tools.

Perhaps you were not cut out to be a witness. The thought of speaking to another person about your beliefs may scare you into silence. But there are other ways to communicate. Can you tell stories? Can you sing? Can you dance? Can you draw? Faith, and the joy it brings you, can be communicated through many means. Offer God the talents you do have, and He will give you a way to use them.

Father, show me how I can tell others
about Your mighty works and pass on
the faith I treasure. You know what I
am capable of, and I do want to help.

Our gifts and attainments are not only to
be light and warmth in our own dwellings,
but are also to shine through the windows
into the dark night, to guide and cheer
bewildered travelers on the road.

HENRY WARD BEECHER

THINK IT OVER

What gifts or talents do you have?

How can you or how do you use them to attract others to God?

In what ways can you develop or strengthen those gifts or talents?

Never underestimate the power
of the gifts that are within you.
Gifts and talents are given to us
not only so that we can fulfill to
the fullest the call in our own lives,
but also so that we can reach the
souls who are attached to those gifts.

JOHN MASON

*For unto every one that hath shall be
given, and he shall have abundance:
but from him that hath not shall be
taken away even that which he hath.*

MATTHEW 25:29

DAY 12

KNOWING THE REWARDS

*For God giveth to a man that is good
in his sight wisdom, and knowledge,
and joy: but to the sinner he giveth travail,
to gather and to heap up, that he may
give to him that is good before God.
This also is vanity and vexation of spirit.*

ECCLESIASTES 2:26

Wisdom, knowledge, and joy are the rewards of those who please God. These rewards come directly from God, with no one in between. What goes around comes around, and the sinner ends up with nothing. Sometimes life doesn't seem to work this way, but a lot goes on that we don't see, and we have to take the Lord's word for it, because this is a long-term promise.

More importantly, Ecclesiastes 2:26 helps us set our priorities. Our most important task is pleasing God with the way we live. If we do this, the rewards will follow. God Himself will provide us with the wisdom, knowledge, and joy we need, and financial rewards will follow from them. Sin, on the other hand, has no long-term rewards at all.

Father, I want to please You with my
life. If my actions result in rewards,
I will be thankful for them, but living
my life according to Your wishes is
the greatest reward of all.

It is His business to lead, command,
impel, send, call, or whatever you want
to call it. It is your business to obey,
follow, move, respond, or what have you.

JIM ELLIOT

Do you find you are more of a people pleaser than a God pleaser?

When has God rewarded you with wisdom, knowledge, and joy—just when you needed them?

How else has God blessed you when you've lived to please Him—and only Him?

It is possible to please God first
and at the same time to please
those around us. But if we always
try to please those around us first,
we will never please God.

RUBYE GOODLETT

*Without faith it is impossible to
please him: for he that cometh
to God must believe that he is,
and that he is a rewarder of
them that diligently seek him.*

HEBREWS 11:6

DAY 13

THE LAW VS. GRACE

Certain men which came down from Judaea taught the brethren, and said, Except ye be circumcised after the manner of Moses, ye cannot be saved.

ACTS 15:1

People—even some well-meaning Christians—have a hard time accepting grace. They can't believe they don't have to add something to God's work. So they set up rules and regulations: "You have to do *this*, or you aren't a Christian." "You don't really love God unless you do *that*."

The men in this verse were trying to follow the Old Testament Law as well as Jesus. They couldn't accept that His blood had done it all and that, when they accepted Him, their hearts, not their bodies, were circumcised. Many serious Gentile believers who wanted to obey God but feared doing something wrong did what these Judaizers said, unnecessarily. Fear led them into sin.

God doesn't want you to be afraid, to worry if you've dotted all the *i*'s and crossed all the *t*'s that will let you enter heaven. No, He loves you, so He gave you a free gift, no strings attached. Enjoy that gift today.

Thank You, Jesus, for Your grace.
You've done everything that had to
be done to bring me into heaven.
I want to give my life as thanks.

Law tells me how crooked I am; grace
comes along and straightens me out.

D. L. MOODY

THINK IT OVER

Have you ever tried to earn God's grace; if so, how?

In what ways, if any, have modern-day Judaizers put fear into your heart?

How does it feel, knowing God has blessed you with grace, regardless of what you've done—or not done?

God's grace is just that—grace,
unmerited favor. Nothing I
will do can ever cause Him
to love me more or less.

DAVID B. HAWKINS, PhD

*For by grace are ye saved through
faith; and that not of yourselves:
it is the gift of God.*

EPHESIANS 2:8

THE POWER OF PRAYER

*My friends scorn me: but mine eye
poureth out tears unto God. O that one
might plead for a man with God, as a
man pleadeth for his neighbour!*

JOB 16:20-21

How do you pray for others? Is it merely, "Bless John, help Jane"? Imagine yourself in God's shoes, listening to such a shopping list of prayer. Pretty boring, isn't it? Hearing such stuff must be harder for Him than praying it is for us.

God's heart breaks when He thinks of all the blessings we could ask for that He would gladly give. But if He gave what we asked, what would that be? Are we looking for healing, peaceful relationships, conversion, or a thousand other things?

We'll never quite know how prayer works to move God's hand. But through the Spirit, who intercedes for us, we can bring to Him the needs of friends, family, and even Christians who live half a world away. Lives begin to change, and we can praise God for His works.

The Spirit intercedes for you every day. Are you interceding for others, too?

Father God, fill me with Your love
for others. Let my prayer time
be a blessing to the world.

Beware in your prayers, above everything
else, of limiting God, not only by unbelief,
but by fancying that you know what He can
do. Expect unexpected things, "above all
that we ask or think." Each time, before you
intercede, be quiet first, and worship God
in His glory. Think of what He can do, and
how He delights to hear the prayers of His
redeemed people. Think of your place and
privilege in Christ, and expect great things!

ANDREW MURRAY

THINK IT OVER

When you are facing difficulties, how does it feel
to know others are praying for you?

How can you use that awareness to empower
your own prayers for others?

In what ways can you make intercessory prayer
feel like a privilege—not an obligation?

When we hold up the life of another
before God, when we expose it to
God's love, when we pray. . .only
then do we sense what it means to
share in God's work, in his concern;
only then do the walls that separate
us from others go down and we sense
that we are at bottom all knit together
in a great and intimate family.

DOUGLAS STEERE

*Putting his hands on him [Ananias]
said, Brother Saul, the Lord, even Jesus,
that appeared unto thee in the way as
thou camest, hath sent me, that thou
mightest receive thy sight, and be filled
with the Holy Ghost. And immediately
there fell from his eyes as it had been
scales: and he received sight forthwith.*

ACTS 9:17–18

DAY 15

FRIENDLY GOSSIP

A froward man soweth strife: and a whisperer separateth chief friends.
PROVERBS 16:28

Finding and keeping good friends is hard work. You go through a lot of acquaintances before you find one friend you can trust totally and be honest with—and then you have to work at staying friends with him or her.

One of the best ways to lose a friend is to listen to "whispers" or gossip: "You know what he said about you?" The only proper answer to this question is, "No, and I don't want to hear about it from you." You never know the intentions of a gossip, and it's foolish to listen to one. If you have a problem with a friend, it should stay between the two of you until you work it out. No third party is going to help. Refuse to listen to gossip about a friend if you value the friendship.

Lord, gossip can sometimes be fun,
but more often it's dangerous. Give me
the good sense to ignore it and deal
honestly with my friends in all things.

Whoever keeps an open ear for tattlers will
be sure to hear the trumpet of contention.

WILLIAM COWPER

THINK IT OVER

When, if ever, have you been tripped up by gossip of your own or that of another?

Why do you think "gossip" is dangerous enough to be catalogued with murder (see Romans 1:29)?

What is your "exit strategy" when someone starts gossiping about a friend?

Gossip is the devil's radio.
GEORGE HARRISON

The words of a talebearer are as wounds, and they go down into the innermost parts of the belly.
PROVERBS 18:8

DAY 16

PROVING YOUR WORTH

*He that is faithful in that which
is least is faithful also in much:
and he that is unjust in the least
is unjust also in much.*

LUKE 16:10

You're just starting off in your job, and nobody trusts you with very much. You do what you're told, day after day, and it gets pretty boring after awhile. Where's the challenge? What do you have to do before you get to make a few decisions or enjoy some responsibility?

Unfortunately, you have to keep on doing what you're doing—only better. You have to master the boring stuff first—really get it down pat—and be the best "nobody" anyone's ever seen. Don't think people aren't watching, because they are. But even boring work has to be done well, and if you sleepwalk through the day, it will be noticed. However, if you prove yourself trustworthy in this job, a better one will be ahead for you. At the very least, you'll end up with a good reference for your resume.

Father, when my work gets so boring I want to nod off about midafternoon, remind me that I hold the keys to my own success in my own hands. I may be a nobody now, but I won't be for long, with Your help.

I seem to have been led little by little, toward my work; and I believe that the same fact will appear in the life of anyone who will cultivate such powers as God has given him, and then go on, bravely, quietly, but persistently, doing such work as comes to his hands.

FANNY CROSBY

What, to you, is the meaning of *success*?

In what ways do you hold the keys to that success?

How can you change your view of work from one of drudgery to one of opportunity?

God honors work.
So honor God in your work.
MAX LUCADO

And whatsoever ye do, do it heartily,
as to the Lord, and not unto men;
Knowing that of the Lord ye shall
receive the reward of the inheritance:
for ye serve the Lord Christ.
COLOSSIANS 3:23-24

DAY 17

WORRYING—AND CONTENTMENT

*Which of you by taking thought can
add one cubit unto his stature?*
MATTHEW 6:27

With a closet full of clothes, we worry about not having "anything" or the "right" thing to wear. With a cupboard full of food, there's still "nothing" to eat. These are minor worries not based on fact, but they continue to nag at us until we go out and buy the "right" clothes or cram the cupboard with enough food to feed a small nation.

Many people have more legitimate worries—actual needs that consume every waking moment in a struggle for survival. What's amazing is that many of these people are still happy, despite their problems. How do they do it? Perhaps they've read a little further in Matthew 6, where Jesus promised, "Seek first his kingdom and his righteousness, and all these things will be given to you as well" (v. 33).

Worry wastes time and produces nothing, while seeking God and His kingdom is always a worthwhile activity that will banish trivial worries and provide us with whatever we need.

Father, I know the rent money will be
there when I need it if I concentrate
on living righteously and don't let my
worries paralyze me. Times may get tough,
but I can make it with Your help.

Seek not great things for yourselves in
this world, for if your garments be too long,
they will make you stumble; and one staff
helps a man in his journey, when many
in his hands at once hinders him.

William Bridge

THINK IT OVER

What, if any, are your main worries?

Why haven't you passed these worries from your shoulders to God's?

What about worry implies less than absolute faith in God?

When you or I worry, we are choosing to be mastered by our circumstances instead of by the truth of God. The vicissitudes and trials of life pale in comparison to the greatness of our salvation. Jesus wants us to realize it doesn't make sense to believe God can save us from eternal hell, but not help us in the practical matters of life.

JOHN MACARTHUR

My soul, wait thou only upon God;
for my expectation is from him.
He only is my rock and my salvation:
he is my defence; I shall not be moved.

PSALM 62:5–6

PREPAREDNESS

*And others had trial of cruel
mockings and scourgings, yea,
moreover of bonds and imprisonment:
They were stoned, they were sawn
asunder, were tempted, were slain
with the sword: they wandered about
in sheepskins and goatskins; being
destitute, afflicted, tormented; (of whom
the world was not worthy).*
HEBREWS 11:36–38

Most of us will never have to face death for our faith, but there are dangers in feeling too safe. For one thing, someone in a safe country never even thinks about martyrdom—personal martyrdom. We aren't prepared for it and have no idea how we would react to that type of danger. What would you do if you had to renounce your faith in order to live? What would you do to keep your children alive? You can't make these decisions wisely and rationally when someone's pointing a gun at your head, and there won't be any chance to change your mind. Think about it now, while there's time—just in case.

Father, I don't even want to think about this happening to me, but give me the strength and the courage to do what I have to do if the time should ever come.

Oh, how much those men are to be valued who, in the spirit with which the widow gave up her two mites, have given up themselves! How their names sparkle! How rich their very ashes are! How they will count up in heaven!

EDWIN HUBBELL CHAPIN

THINK IT OVER

For what or whom are you willing to give up
your life?

What does it mean "to live is Christ" (see
Philippians 1:21)?

How can you support those who may one day
have to sacrifice their lives for their faith?

He is no fool who gives up
what he cannot keep to gain
what he cannot lose.

Jim Elliot

*For to me to live is Christ,
and to die is gain.*

Philippians 1:21

HONING OUR HEARING

Thine ears shall hear a word behind thee, saying, This is the way, walk ye in it, when ye turn to the right hand, and when ye turn to the left.

ISAIAH 30:21

God has not left us alone on the earth to struggle through our lives without guidance. Whether we call it God's voice or our own conscience, it is there to help us. We have the freedom to ignore the voice and go our own way. There are no marionette strings attached to us that God pulls to keep us on the path. He will tell us which way to go, but we control our own actions.

The same thing happens to parents who raise their children properly and then can do nothing but watch when something goes wrong and their children turn to drugs or crime. Imagine the pain those parents feel and then multiply it to infinity to begin to understand a fraction of the pain we must cause our heavenly Father.

Don't let the world's uproar drown out the voice you hear behind you. It's the best friend you will ever have.

Father, I want to follow Your path.
Help me listen when You guide
me in the way I should go.

Conscience is thoroughly well-bred
and soon leaves off talking to
those who do not wish to hear it.

Samuel Butler

THINK IT OVER

How do you settle yourself in order to hear God speaking to you?

What results when you follow your conscience?

How does it feel when you ignore God's voice and go your own way?

Conscience is the soul of freedom,
its eyes, its energy, its life. Without
conscience, freedom never knows
what to do with itself.

THOMAS MERTON

*Pray for us: for we trust we have
a good conscience, in all things
willing to live honestly.*

HEBREWS 13:18

THE RIGHT KIND OF SERVICE

*Therefore all things whatsoever
ye would that men should do to you,
do ye even so to them: for this is the
law and the prophets.*

MATTHEW 7:12

Jana sat in the crowded doctor's office, miserable with a head cold and barely paying attention to her surroundings. If only she could get in to see the doctor and get home and to bed!

She barely noticed the grimacing man across from her until another patient told the nurse, "He's in more pain than I am. Please take him first."

Jana admired the woman, but guilt stabbed her heart. *I never realized he was in such pain,* she thought. *If I had, would I have done the same, even though it meant a longer wait?*

Doing good for others—especially those outside our circle of friends—means tuning into their needs. Do we block ourselves behind a pseudospiritual wall and a "don't touch" mentality? Or do we open up to others, talk to hurting people, and offer them Jesus' help?

After all, that's only a small part of what He gave us.

Jesus, reaching out is hard when I get boxed into myself. Open my heart and eyes so I can help others.

The idea that service to God should have only to do with a church altar, singing, reading, sacrifice, and the like is without doubt but the worst trick of the devil. How could the devil have led us more effectively astray than by the narrow conception that service to God takes place only in a church and by the works done therein?

MARTIN LUTHER

THINK IT OVER

How would the world change if we all had a servant's heart?

What can you do to increase your awareness of the needs of those around you—in every part of your day?

Who can you serve today?

A life that selflessly and
sacrificially serves the least is
a worthy goal worth pursuing.
LESLIE LUDY

*Whosoever will be great among
you, let him be your minister;
and whosoever will be chief among
you, let him be your servant.*
MATTHEW 20:26–27

DAY 21

THE MUSIC DEBATE

Serve the LORD with gladness: come
before his presence with singing.
PSALM 100:2

S ome music sounds good to you—and some is just irritating noise. But your "noise" is another person's "sounds good."

Church music is part of the "noise"-"sounds good" debate. If your congregation likes the "oldies and moldies" of Christian music and you like the latest tunes on the Christian music shelves, you may be tempted to hold your ears during services. Worse, those slow, dull songs may lull you to sleep.

Maybe the music you can't stand is favored by your pastor or music leader. Maybe other church members have encouraged the music director to play it. And asking anyone to change the music style could start World War III.

This psalm doesn't mention the kind of music churches should play—it doesn't specify classical, pop, rock music, or even Old Testament–style music. That's because the music itself isn't important— worshipping God is. He deserves our praise, no matter what the song is. A joyful heart can always praise Him.

Whether or not your church is tuned in to your music style, sing with all your heart.

Lord, I want to praise You, not start
a war. Thank You for music I enjoy.
Let me sing Your praises today.

The only music minister to whom the Lord
will say, "Well done, thou good and faithful
servant," is the one whose life proves what
their lyrics are saying, and to whom music
is the least important part of their life.
Glorifying the only worthy One has to be
a minister's most important goal!

KEITH GREEN

THINK IT OVER

Which style of Christian music do you most enjoy? Why?

When music other than your preferred style is being played, how do you react?

How can you find joy in worshipping the Lord no matter what type of music is being performed?

Worship is a personal encounter with God in which one expresses love for God, concentrates on His attributes, and brings the focus back to Him.

JAMES A. SCUDDER

Let the word of Christ dwell in you richly in all wisdom; teaching and admonishing one another in psalms and hymns and spiritual songs, singing with grace in your hearts to the Lord.

COLOSSIANS 3:16

DAY 22

UNDER COVER

Thou [Ananias] hast not lied
unto men, but unto God.
ACTS 5:4

Okay, so maybe you aren't like Ananias. You've never lied about how much money you had to give. But are you honest with God?

That's tough. After all, to be totally honest with God means letting Him inside those deep, dark places no one else knows about. The date that was going so well, until. . . Your real thoughts about that coworker. . . The way you really feel about things in His Word.

We'd like to hide from God. Our messy lives just don't seem good enough for Him. The problem is, until we open up to Him, we'll never change. God doesn't barge into our hearts, ferreting out sin. Instead, He woos us, shows us the right path, and invites us to give up those dark holes in our lives.

If we don't, we may not get suddenly wiped out, like Ananias, but a slow spiritual death creeps into our lives. Is it creeping into your life?

Lord, it's hard to be honest with someone
as holy as You. But I want to be like
You in this, too. Cleanse my heart.

Character is what you
are in the dark.

D. L. MOODY

What, if anything, is keeping you from being
totally open with God?

How would it improve your spiritual life if you
were honest with the Lord—about *everything*?

How will you feel when you bring God's light
into your hidden corners?

Always meet with God as a God who
desires truth in the inward parts.
In all your confession of sin, in all
your religion, in your whole existence,
let truth in the inward parts be your
desire, as it is the desire of God.

ANDREW MURRAY

*Behold, thou desirest truth in the
inward parts: and in the hidden part
thou shalt make me to know wisdom.*

PSALM 51:6

DAY 23

TRUSTING HIM

He is the Rock, his work is perfect:
for all his ways are judgment:
a God of truth and without iniquity,
just and right is he.

DEUTERONOMY 32:4

Wise men and women have wrestled with this verse for centuries, so it's not unusual for the average person to ask the obvious question: If God is just, why isn't His world? Why don't the good prosper and the evil fail? Why do starvation and genocide still rage today?

One obvious answer is that God is working with flawed materials—us. Over the course of history, we've changed the world, but not always for the better. He gave us dominion over the earth, and our sin has corrupted a perfectly just situation.

Maybe the best answer to the just-God/unjust-world problem is to admit that we simply don't know what's going on. We're not seeing the whole picture. Even if we could, we probably wouldn't understand it. Some things we just have to take on faith. God is still in the world, doing what only He can do.

Father, I place my life in Your hands,
certain that all things work according to
Your will, whether I understand or not.

Never be afraid to trust an
unknown future to a known God.

CORRIE TEN BOOM

THINK IT OVER

What seeming injustices keep you up at night?

What "wrongs" are within your power to make "right"?

What do you need to do to replace your uncertainty of the future with a trust of God in the present?

May the peace which no earthly disturbance can mar, which is of the Father through His inspiration and love, fill your hearts, and enable you to go on in the journey of life with a feeling of trust and confidence that nothing can disturb.

LELAND STANFORD

Thou wilt keep him in perfect peace, whose mind is stayed on thee: because he trusteth in thee.

ISAIAH 26:3

FAIR-WEATHER FRIENDS

*And as they sat and did eat, Jesus
said, Verily I say unto you, One of you
which eateth with me shall betray
me. And they began to be sorrowful,
and to say unto him one by one,
Is it I? and another said, Is it I?*

MARK 14:18–19

Just the kind of firm believers you'd like to have following you if you were about to face the cross, right? Twelve men who aren't even sure of their own hearts! Told that one would betray Jesus, for a single, honest moment, not one disciple—not even brash Peter—guaranteed he would never give in.

But Jesus used these less-than-confident men precisely because they recognized their own weaknesses. God doesn't look for self-sufficient disciples who never err. He looks for those who know they are weak and know whom to turn to—Jesus.

If you're facing trouble and feel you lack the strength to stand firm, don't waste your time worrying; turn to Jesus instead. You're in exactly the right place.

Lord Jesus, I'm so weak that sometimes
I don't even realize it. When I face
a cross, I can trust only in You.

So let it be in God's own might
We gird us for the coming fight,
And, strong in Him whose cause is ours
In conflict with unholy powers,
We grasp the weapons he has given,
The Light, and Truth, and Love of Heaven.

JOHN GREENLEAF WHITTIER

THINK IT OVER

What do you consider to be some of your
weaknesses?

_____

_____

_____

_____

When have you been "at the end of yourself"?

_____

_____

_____

How does it feel to know that, in Jesus, you are
given the power to do the unimaginable?

_____

_____

_____

No matter what limitation or circumstance you find yourself up against in life, there is a God who can empower you and gift you to go past what you thought was possible. . .when you're at the end of yourself, that's the time he can do his best work.

HENRY CLOUD AND JOHN TOWNSEND

We have this treasure in earthen vessels, that the excellency of the power may be of God, and not of us.

2 CORINTHIANS 4:7

BUILDING UP

*Then said I unto them, Ye see
the distress that we are in,
how Jerusalem lieth waste,
and the gates thereof are burned
with fire: come, and let us build
up the wall of Jerusalem,
that we be no more a reproach.*

NEHEMIAH 2:17

Overcome with discouragement, the Jews who had returned to Jerusalem from exile huddled in a city open to invaders. Broken walls surrounded what was left of the city, and even its gates were burned. But no one started a citywide rebuilding project.

When Nehemiah heard of the situation, instead of hunkering down in fear, he got permission to rebuild the walls. He traveled to Jerusalem, inspected the site, and confronted the people. Encouragement and a plan were all the people needed—and Nehemiah gave them both.

Every Christian needs lifting up. When job hunting gets you down, it's great to have someone show you the ropes and say something heartening. If you're struggling with sin, a seasoned Christian can share how he or she overcame the same temptation.

Don't let discouragement get the best of you. Reach out for help!

When I feel lower than a snake,
Lord, it's hard to tell others.
Help me reach out for help.

There are high spots in all of our lives,
and most of them have come about through
encouragement from someone else.

GEORGE MATTHEW ADAMS

THINK IT OVER

Who is the biggest encourager in your life right now?

Which Bible verses fill you with encouragement from God?

What will you do today to encourage someone else?

Encouragement is not a technique
to be mastered; it is a sensitivity to
people and a confidence in God that
must be nourished and demonstrated.

LARRY CRABB

*Have not I commanded thee?
Be strong and of a good courage;
be not afraid, neither be thou
dismayed: for the LORD thy God is
with thee whithersoever thou goest.*

JOSHUA 1:9

DAY 26

DEALING WITH ANGER

*He that is soon angry
dealeth foolishly.*
PROVERBS 14:17

People handle anger in various ways. Some manage to push it down and continue as if they never felt it (probably giving themselves ulcers in the process). Others kick chairs in private but soon come to terms with their anger. Still others blow up and immediately feel better. We tend to react to anger the same way our parents did.

In the same way, we all have different boiling points. It takes a lot to get some people angry, while others erupt at the slightest provocation.

However you react to anger, you need to maintain control. Anger makes us stupid. We do and say things we would never do under normal circumstances, starting fistfights or saying words we can never take back.

When anger takes over, get away if you can't control your emotions. Go hide out in the restroom, if necessary. Shut a door behind you until you are back in control. A real man does not hit. A strong woman asserts control over herself, not over others.

Father, when I want to strike out in anger, whether verbally or physically, give me the self-control I need to avoid doing anything stupid.

The best time for you to hold your tongue is the time you feel you must say something or bust.

Josh Billings

THINK IT OVER

How do you express your anger?

What has resulted when, if ever, you allowed
rage to control your actions and words?

What outlets—walking it off, smashing tennis
balls, etc.—do you find for your anger?

Anger is like a homemade bomb strapped around one's waist. Whoever detonates the bomb becomes a suicide bomber. They not only injure anyone in the near vicinity, but they go up as well. Anger destroys their reputation, devastates friendships and, worst of all amputates their potential.

WAYNE CORDEIRO

A wrathful man stirreth up strife: but he that is slow to anger appeaseth strife.

PROVERBS 15:18

DAY 27

PLAYING THE FOOL

*The fool hath said in his heart,
There is no God. They are corrupt,
they have done abominable works,
there is none that doeth good.*

PSALM 14:1

We may call ourselves a fool when we spill milk or forget to pick something up at the store. We should have known better, but we just weren't paying attention. Yet this sort of carelessness isn't the kind of foolishness God talks about in His Word. When God calls someone a fool, He's very serious. In scripture, fools are those who don't believe in Him.

To God, anyone who ignores the obvious messages He's given the world is missing more than mental focus. Real foolish thinking—such as self-centeredness and disregard for right—steeps a person in wickedness. Apart from God, no one does good.

We don't need to be hard on ourselves when we forget to pick up bread at the grocery store, but we do need to be careful that we don't emulate the works of the truly foolish—those who don't believe God even exists.

Lord, any goodness I do comes
from You. When others deny You,
I want to stand firm in faith instead
of acting as if You don't exist.

As a vessel is known by the sound,
whether it be cracked or not;
so men are proved, by their speeches,
whether they be wise or foolish.

DEMOSTHENES

When, if ever, have you shied away from
vocalizing your beliefs?

What are some other ways you can demonstrate
to the world that you are a believer?

How does it feel knowing that, because of Christ
living through you, you can "do good" in this
world?

It is an honor to believe what the
lips of Jesus taught. I had sooner
be a fool with Christ than a wise
man with the philosophers.

<small>CHARLES SPURGEON</small>

*For the preaching of the cross is
to them that perish foolishness;
but unto us which are saved
it is the power of God.*

<small>1 CORINTHIANS 1:18</small>

UNDER THE INFLUENCE

*Be not deceived: evil communications
corrupt good manners.*
1 CORINTHIANS 15:33

The world is full of "bad company" we can't avoid. The best we can do is recognize ne'er-do-wells for what they are and not let them influence our personal lives.

We do have a voice concerning who we choose to hang around with, but since it takes time to really know a person, we also make mistakes. Sometimes we become friends with someone who is fun to be with, who eases our loneliness—but we soon discover we really don't like some of the things going on. We want to break off the relationship, but that's hard. "Maybe it's not really all that serious." "Maybe I can change him."

It's at this point, when we begin rationalizing insupportable behavior, that our good character becomes corrupted. We overlook one flaw after another until we can no longer say, "This is wrong. I can't do this." A corrupt person is one who can't see the difference between good and bad.

Father, give me the wisdom to choose
my friends carefully, and when I make a
mistake, give me the courage to break off
the relationship before I begin to think
and act like a corrupt person myself.

No man is the whole of himself;
his friends are the rest of him.

HARRY EMERSON FOSDICK

THINK IT OVER

When, if ever, has a so-called friend led you
down the wrong path?

_____

_____

_____

_____

What attributes would you use to describe a
good and godly friend?

_____

_____

_____

_____

Who is your closest friend? Why?

_____

_____

_____

_____

Show me a man's closest companions
and I can make a fairly accurate guess
as to what sort of man he is, as well as
what sort of man he is likely to become.
HOWARD AND WILLIAM HENDRICKS

Iron sharpeneth iron;
so a man sharpeneth the
countenance of his friend.
PROVERBS 27:17

DANGEROUS DABBLING

*I will cut off. . .them that worship the
host of heaven upon the housetops.*
ZEPHANIAH 1:4-5

B ut the occult is dangerous," Brendan warned his church group. "Why—"

Another group member quickly cut him off, pooh-poohing his words. Some in the study didn't want to admit that reading a horoscope was unbiblical.

Knowing Christ isn't a cheap guarantee that you can do anything you like and still spend eternity in heavenly bliss. Dabbling in astrology, palm reading, and tarot cards isn't something God ignores in His people.

Through Zephaniah, God reprimanded the people of Judah for a similar divided allegiance. He never said that they didn't give Him a piece of their lives. They did— but they held on to Baal worship, too. They looked to the stars for answers as well as going to the temple.

God doesn't save a piece of your life; He saves all of it. A faithful response is to give Him your whole life in return. You can't do that if you're also trying to use occult methods to see what the future holds.

You may not know your whole future, but you know who holds it. Trust in Him.

Thank You, Lord, for holding my future.
I want to trust You for everything.

Many do not recognize the fact as they
ought, that Satan has got men fast asleep
in sin and that it is his great device to keep
them so. He does not care what we do if he
can do that. We may sing songs about the
sweet by and by, preach sermons, and say
prayers until doomsday, and he will never
concern himself about us if we don't wake
anybody up. But if we awake the sleeping
sinner, he will gnash on us with his teeth.
This is our work—to wake people up.

Catherine Booth

THINK IT OVER

When and in what situations, if any, have you perceived the evils of the occult?

Why do you think people are attracted to fortune tellers, astrology, numerology, etc.?

In what ways can you help others understand the dangers of following someone or something other than God?

It is to Christ that spiritual truth-seekers must look. Occultism presents nothing but a distraction.

RICHARD ABANES

Therefore hearken not ye to your prophets, nor to your diviners, nor to your dreamers, nor to your enchanters, nor to your sorcerers, which speak unto you. . .for they prophesy a lie unto you.

JEREMIAH 27:9–10

CHARACTER COUNTS

Who can find a virtuous woman?
for her price is far above rubies.
PROVERBS 31:10

When you date someone, do you look for the best-looking girl around, the guy with the most money—or a person with good character? Dreams of your future spouse probably include a great-looking person, romantic evenings together, and wonderful conversations. You may not imagine a man who's truthful or a woman who treats her parents with respect.

God doesn't say you can't marry a good-looking mate or even one with a hefty bank account, but you could live without those. You can't live happily with a weak character. Character doesn't look glamorous. You can't show off by sending your friend a picture of it... but you can live with it for a lifetime. You'll never worry where your mate is when you know he's trustworthy. You'll never fear a family get-together when you know she'll treat your parents kindly.

Is your date a *noble* character—or just a character?

Lord, character may not be the asset I'm dreaming of, but I know it's important. Turn my heart toward someone with a strong love for You and the willingness to do right.

You must look into people, as well as at them.

LORD CHESTERFIELD

What character traits should you look for in a
mate?

In what ways can you keep yourself from being
sucked in by looks and overlooking character
flaws?

How would you describe your ideal, happily-
ever-after mate?

While getting to know each other takes time, it's important to make every effort in the earliest stages of a relationship to show your true self to someone with whom you want to build a close relationship.

LES PARROTT III

The tree is known by his fruit.

MATTHEW 12:33

DAY 31

RENEWAL

Therefore we are buried with him by baptism into death: that like as Christ was raised up from the dead by the glory of the Father, even so we also should walk in newness of life.

ROMANS 6:4

You may have been a Christian for a while, with that brand-new, clean feeling of new faith now slowly evaporating. You don't feel new anymore. *Maybe,* you ponder, *"new" is only for baby Christians. I know I've made "progress,"* you encourage yourself. *I'm not the same person I was before I knew Jesus. But something's missing.*

God didn't make Jesus new for a day, week, or month and then let Him get "old" again. He eternally raised Him from the dead, so through baptism we can share His new life forever.

If vibrant faith has left you, some "old" things probably tarnish your new life. Legalistic or critical attitudes, disobedience, and doubt take the shine off a once-new faith, until you barely know you've been changed.

But repentance during a let's-clear-the-air time with God returns the "new" to eternal life. Spend time with Him in prayer.

Empty me of old things that keep me apart from You, Lord. I want to spend every new day close by Your side.

Do not have your concert first and then tune your instrument afterwards. Begin the day with the Word of God and prayer, and get first of all into harmony with Him.

HUDSON TAYLOR

THINK IT OVER

What things do you need to admit to God?

Which Bible verses could you memorize to get spiritually recharged?

What else can you do to increase your hunger and thirst for God and His Word?

Let me tell you that God,
who began a good work in you,
is not about to stop now.
Jim Cymbala and Dean Merrill

Create in me a clean heart, O God;
and renew a right spirit within me.
Psalm 51:10